INDIANS AT HOME

INDIANS AT HOME

WRITTEN AND ILLUSTRATED BY

ROBERT HOFSINDE

(GRAY-WOLF)

WILLIAM MORROW AND COMPANY • NEW YORK • 1964

By the Same Author:

THE INDIAN AND THE BUFFALO

THE INDIAN AND HIS HORSE

INDIAN BEADWORK

INDIAN FISHING AND CAMPING

INDIAN GAMES AND CRAFTS

INDIAN HUNTING

INDIAN PICTURE WRITING

INDIAN SIGN LANGUAGE

THE INDIAN'S SECRET WORLD

Fifth Printing, May, 1967

To
DON AND JANET
with love

Contents

■ ALGONQUIAN ∽

▥ IROQUOIAN ∽

▤ SIOUAN ∽

▧ ATHABASKAN ∽

▦ ISOLATED LANGUAGES ∽ NW + SE.

1
Indian Homes

WHEN the white man settled the American continent, he pushed the Indian from his home and homeland. He discovered then that the Indian was a family man and would fight to protect his home. We usually think of this home as a picturesque, stately tepee, with a buffalo-hide covering, smoke flaps, and graceful poles extending to the sky. However, the tepee was the home of the Plains Indian only.

9

The Indians built many types of homes. They varied in size, shape, and material, depending on the geographical location of the tribe. What was practical in one section of the country was often not suited to another. For example, sun-dried adobe bricks, made from clay and grasses, were used by the Pueblo Indians of the Southwest to construct their homes, because the bricks stood up well in a dry climate. But if the Northwest Coast Indians had used adobe for their homes, the long rainy season would have soon destroyed them. In other sections of the country wood, bark, earth, brush, grasses, and skins were some of the materials used by the various tribes to make their home shelters.

Before the arrival of the horse, Indian villages were more permanent, and most tribes knew only their closest neighbors. In such an area as, for example, the eastern woodlands, the tribal culture was much the same and the people spoke a similar language. Today the anthropologists have divided American Indians into linguistic groups. The locations of these groups are shown on the shaded map, and in the back of the book is a list of the tribes that belong to each one.

In the following chapters we shall visit some typical tribes and see how they built their homes and how they lived in them.

2
The Algonquian
Wigwam

THE great north woods of the United States and
Canada has been the home of the Ojibwa, who belong to the Algonquian-speaking Indians, for at
least five thousand years. The Ojibwa rarely lived
in a tribal group. To obtain food, they split up into
smaller groups and roamed the forests and the
waterways, hunting and fishing. They were at one
with nature, feeling a closeness with the rocks and
the waters, with the trees, plants, birds, and ani-

mals around them. At times an Ojibwa camp consisted of only a man and his wife, their children,
and the man's parents. Such a life of isolation
made the family depend very strongly upon the
resourcefulness of each person.

The Ojibwa families built four different kinds
of homes. In winter they might live in either a
domed wigwam or one with a peaked roof. In
summer their home was a rectangular bark hut or
a conical-shaped lodge, covered with bark slabs or
with animal skins. But of all the Ojibwa lodges
used, the domed winter wigwam, set in a pine-
sheltered woodland clearing, was the most permanent structure. It had a framework of long, slender
poles and was covered with reed mats and bark.

To build this wigwam, an Indian marked off the
rectangular floor area first. Then, with a stone-
headed club and a pointed hardwood stick, he
made a number of evenly spaced holes in the
ground all along the marked outline. When the
holes were deep enough, he placed the bottom,
or butt, end of a slender, springy pole in each one.
He put long poles along the two short sides of the

rectangle and shorter poles along the two long sides. Then he reached up and pulled one of the poles downward and inward. One man held this pole down, and another pulled down the top of the pole opposite it. While his helper held them in place, the Indian lashed the tops of the poles together with strips of spruce root or with green basswood fibers. Two by two, the poles were bound together, first the short ones that formed the long

walls, then the longer ones that formed the short walls. The result was a large, domed, oval-shaped frame.

Continuing to work together, the men now lashed more saplings to the framework, some going over the roof and others horizontally around the sides. While the work on the frame progressed, the women wove wide flat mats from cattail rushes. When enough of these mats had been made, they covered the wigwam frame with them. Starting from the bottom and working up, they fastened the mats to the framework in an overlapping pattern that prevented rain from seeping in.

To make the wigwam even warmer and more waterproof, the Ojibwa added large slabs of birch, ash, or elm bark as an outer wall. In the center of the roof they left an opening, which would serve as a smoke hole. In bad weather they could close it off with an extra slab of bark.

In one of the short walls the builder kept a space open between the horizontal poles for a doorway, which he later covered with a curtain of tanned deer hide and a big slab of bark. The northern winters are cold, and as a further protection against Old Cold Maker, the north wind, the women wove more reed mats and hung them on the inside walls as an extra lining.

In the middle of the floor, the builder dug a shallow pit and lined it with flat rocks. This was his fireplace. In order to have a steady, warming blaze going day and night, the Ojibwa Indians used the old, and still reliable, star fire. First they

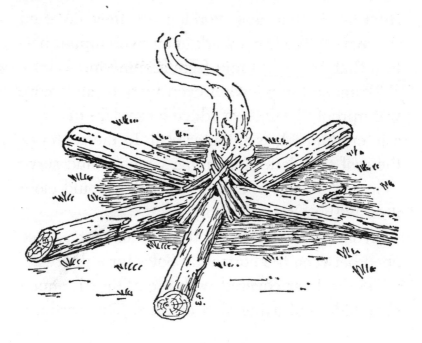

built a small fire in the center of the pit. Then, when it was burning well, they placed five long and solid logs around the central fire. They arranged them so that the logs fanned out from the center like a five-pointed star, with one end of each log resting in the fire. As they burned away, the Indians pushed them back into the fire. When it was stormy or especially cold, the grandfather or grandmother sat up all night to keep the blaze alive.

Within these permanent winter wigwams, the Ojibwa built sleeping platforms, which usually ran the full length of the two long walls. Made from poles and saplings, they were raised from twelve to fourteen inches above the ground. By night they served as beds, but during the day they became seats, tables, or workbenches as the need arose. The Indians spread their ever-useful reed mats over the bed shelves and left them there at all times. During the night they slept between bear or caribou robes. In the morning they rolled up the bedding and stored it under the shelf platforms.

When the fall days began to turn crisp and to smell as if snow would soon come, the children went into the woods, gathered up fallen pine needles, and put them in a large birch-bark box. Then they carried the needles back to the wigwam and spread them on the floor in a thick, even layer. After many trips for needles, the children at last had the entire floor space covered, up to within a few inches of the fire. Their mother spread some of her reed mats over the needles, and this covering helped a great deal to keep the earthen floor warm.

Sometimes the Ojibwa spent their winters in a house with a peaked roof. It, too, was covered with mats and bark, but it was shaped much like a large pup tent. When cutting the frame poles for it, the builder left forked branches on near the top. He then set up the poles in pairs so that they leaned toward each other and the forks interlocked. After the poles were up, he ran a long ridgepole along these forks.

The family then rested more poles and saplings against the ridgepole until they formed two slant-

ing walls. Finally they covered the whole structure with mats and a layer of bark slabs, which
were held in place with a few more poles resting
against the walls from the outside.

Peaked-roof lodges often had doorways, covered with tanned hides, in both the front and the
back.

The Ojibwa home belonged to the woman, and
her work centered around it. However, much of
the man's work was also carried on at home. He
made his fishing and hunting gear there and
worked constantly to keep his spears, arrows,
bows, nets, and snares in good repair.

When game was plentiful and the larder well
stocked with venison, dried and smoked fish,
waterfowl, wild rice, and maple syrup, then the
family could stay in and around the lodge together. They spent long winter evenings by the
fire. The daughter might play with her buckskin
doll, while her mother carefully peeled the outer
layer of birch bark from a box, creating a picture
of moose and other animals out of the darker under

bark. The son of the family might chip away on a piece of flint, trying his hand at arrow making, while his father mended a broken piece of webbing on one of his snowshoes.

The family circle also included the grandparents, and while the rest worked Grandfather told stories from the past. They were tales of Indian life and of the forest, tales of great feats performed by outstanding men of the tribe, tales to spur the young boy to good deeds and to help keep alive the old traditions of the people.

But good as these evenings were, the family longed for the winter moons to end, for the snows to melt, and for spring to awaken the earth once again. When spring did arrive and the weather became warmer, the family moved outdoors. There they had an outside fire for cooking, and against one side of the wigwam they built a wide, porchlike shelf, with a roof of bark or mats. Much of the women's daily work took place here. Sitting on this platform, they might, for example, work dyed porcupine quills into a fine floral pattern on a buckskin garment.

With the coming of spring to the North, the Ojibwa family moved away from their winter home. They removed the bark and the mats from the wigwam, but left the frame standing. The wigwam covers were flexible enough to be rolled up like a rug and then stowed in the bottom of a canoe, ready for use at the new campsite. Now the lonely living of the Ojibwa was interrupted for a time. Each year as many as fifteen families gathered at one camp to tap the maple trees for their sap and to boil the sap into maple syrup. The custom produced much visiting, exchange of news, and gossip.

Before spring actually blossomed into early summer, the encampment broke up, and each family departed for its own hunting and fishing grounds. When the family planned to spend several weeks in one place during the summer, they usually constructed a rectangular-shaped hut. This dwelling had straight walls and a peaked roof, and it was covered with the mats and bark the family had brought with them. When the family planned to stay overnight only, they often erected a conical, or tepee-shaped, shelter. The builder set up a number of tepee poles, which interlocked at the peak. From floor to peak measured between six and ten feet. The floor diameter ranged from twelve to sixteen feet. Usually the family covered the frame with a thick layer of pine branches, but if they planned to stay longer, they used the reed mats instead.

The Ojibwa were among the first Indian tribes to meet white men, especially those in search of furs. Soon these woodland people found a steady market for their fine furs and, with the establishment of trading posts, were able to obtain a good many of the white man's timesaving articles. Guns, good knives, iron kettles, and wool blankets eased their burden at home and on the hunting trail.

3
The Iroquois Longhouse

THE longhouse of the Iroquois was a symbol of their confederacy, and it was represented as extending from the Hudson River to Lake Erie. Its walls sheltered the five original tribes: the Mohawks, the Senecas, the Oneidas, the Cayugas, and the Onondagas. Each tribe had certain duties within the longhouse. The Mohawks were the doorkeepers of the eastern end of the longhouse and tended the fire there. The Senecas performed the same tasks at the western end. Between the eastern fire and the center was a third fire, kept by the Oneidas, and between the western fire and the center was a fourth, kept by the Cayugas. The Onondagas tended the ever-burning central fire and also presided over the council of the League of the Iroquois. This league of five nations later became six when they took in the Tuscaroras. They all belonged to the Iroquoian linguistic group, and they all were woodland people.

While the Ojibwa lived in single-family wigwams, the Iroquois built large community dwellings, known as longhouses, and lived together in great villages. The longhouses varied in size, and sheltered from five to twenty families. They were from fifteen to twenty-five feet wide and from thirty to two hundred feet long, rising to a height of fifteen or twenty feet at the peak of the roof. The villages also varied in size. Each settlement contained from twelve to a hundred longhouses, and was surrounded by a tall, stout stockade, which protected the villagers from their centuries-old enemy, the Algonquians.

The Iroquois needed a good many trees, both young and old, to build a longhouse. Sometimes they used basswood, ash, or cedar, but they preferred elm, which was best to work with in spring or early summer.

Although the Iroquois had only stone axes and stone-headed clubs with which to cut down the trees, they used a method that somewhat simplified this work. While some of the men cut down slender trees for framework and rafters, others began the work of felling the larger trees from which they would obtain bark for roof and wall coverings. First they made a solid ring of clay around the trunk of a tree, just a few feet above the ground. Then they leaned dry branches against the tree below the clay ring and set them on fire. As the branches burned, the men added more fuel until the bark on the bottom of the tree became quite charred. They chopped away this charred part with their stone tools, and then they started a new fire. The men chopped some more, burned some more. Hour after hour they worked until at last the tree came crashing down. The ring of clay around the trunk prevented the fire from extending above it.

For days the men and boys worked, and at last they had the trees down, had limbed them and peeled off the bark. The bark slabs were four feet wide and from six to eight feet long. After the Indians removed them from the trees, they stacked them on top of each other and weighted them down with rocks or logs to keep them from warping.

Next the men marked off the outline of the actual floor space of the building and dug holes along it. Into the holes they set upright poles, with forked limbs on top. Then, using the inner bark from basswood or hickory as a lashing material, they fastened horizontal poles around the framework of uprights. Because they weighed less, the young boys climbed up and placed other poles in the forks of the uprights, so they extended across from wall to wall, and lashed them down firmly. These poles served as rafters. The roof was peaked, yet it had no ridgepole. The men slanted roof supports toward each other in pairs, so that the slender

ends crossed at the top. They bent the ends a little and lashed them together, forming a slight curve.

By now the large slabs of bark were dry. The women placed them in a line on the ground so that each one overlapped the next. Then, with a sharp bone awl, they punched holes through the tops and strung the slabs together with basswood cordage. In this manner, they added slab after slab until they had a long runner of bark. Starting at the bottom of the house and working lengthwise, the men lashed the runners to the outside of the frame. Each layer slightly overlapped the one laid on below it.

To hold the bark in place more securely, the men lashed more poles to the outside. For this task, they had to work in pairs, with one man inside the building and another outside. First they set the outer pole against the original inside pole. Then they punched two holes through the bark wall, one on each side of the poles. The man outside passed each end of a basswood cord through one pair of holes to the man inside, who pulled the ends up and knotted them firmly. Since all the

31

men and boys worked on the framework, it was not long before the job was completed.

The Iroquois entered a longhouse from either end through a roomy vestibule that was as wide as the house and about twelve feet deep. They used these two end rooms for storage and as a place for visiting. When summer came, they converted the rooms into open porches by removing the bark slabs from the sides. In the winter they closed the outer doorway with a deer hide or with a bark-slab door, hung on wooden hinges.

The people built fires, which were needed both for cooking and for light, in the center of the longhouse from end to end. Some of the largest longhouses had as many as twelve such fireplaces. There were no windows, but a good deal of light came through the smoke holes in the roof. During snowy or rainy weather the Indians covered the smoke holes with additional bark slabs, which they pushed into place from the inside with the aid of long poles. At such times the interior was dark and smoke-filled, making the home very uncomfortable.

When a house became too smoky, about the only thing the people could do to escape the discomfort was to retire to the family sleeping shelves, which they built eighteen inches from the floor against the two long walls. Each family had a space eight to twelve feet long and from five to six feet deep. Both ends were walled off with bark slabs for privacy. The Iroquois hung sweet grass on the partitions, both as a decoration and as a perfume, for this grass, as the name implies, gives off a pleasing fragrance, especially when damp.

Above each sleeping area the Indians built still another shelf supported by poles that rested on the partitions. Here they stored their personal belongings, such as bark boxes, pottery, snowshoes, and hunting gear. The front pole that held this shelf up also served as a rod for curtains of tanned deer hides, which covered the front opening of the sleeping platform. The space below the platform held the family cooking pots, carved spoons, and water bowls.

The rafters of the longhouse were hung with corn, the husks braided together, and with strings of dried apples, pumpkins, squash, and other fruits of the fields. In the two end vestibules and the spaces between some of the sleeping platforms, the people stored dried meat and fish. For such storage, the men made large bark barrels, lined with untanned deer hides, which kept the food fresh.

The Indians used the cornhusks as kindling and as a stuffing for pillows and mattresses. Dried corn-

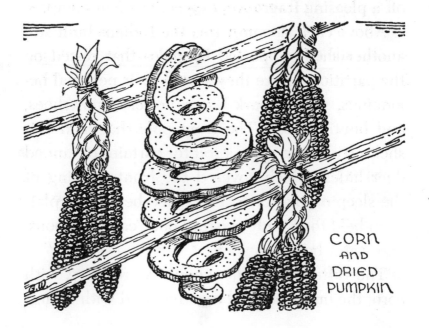

CORN
AND
DRIED
PUMPKIN

cobs served as fuel, as scrubbing brushes for clean-
ing clay pots and wooden dishes, and sometimes
as back scratchers.

Two families usually shared the same fire, and
their companionship was a pleasant one. Here, at
the end of a day, the men sat down to smoke
and talk. Here, too, they made or repaired their
weapons and the things they needed on the game
trail. While the men worked on their crafts the
women worked on tasks such as replacing broken
pottery bowls. An Iroquois woman made a bowl
so that she could stand it in the fire when cooking
and hang it up when she was not using it. She
looped a bark cord, with a handle attached, around
the bowl just below the lip, or upper rim, which
folded outward. The lip prevented the cord from
slipping off the top. So the bowl would remain
upright when set in the hot coals, she made it with
a pointed bottom. When a woman put such a pot
on to boil, she gave it a deft twist to left or right,
which dug it firmly into the ashes.

An Iroquois woman also had time at home for

her own grooming. She brushed her hair with a combination comb and hairbrush made from the tail of a porcupine, and oiled it with a tonic of sun-flower-seed oil, parting it in a neat, straight line through the middle. Unmarried girls wore their hair in two long braids and streaked the center part with vermilion. Married women wore only one braid at the nape of the neck. They then doubled this braid back on itself and held it in

place with a quill-embroidered buckskin band. An Iroquois woman also used face powder and rouge. She made the powder, which was reddish in color, by pulverizing the dry-rotted inner parts of pine trees. By carefully cutting off a soft, fluffy cattail head that she found at the water's edge, she had a powder puff with a built-in handle. She obtained rouge by splitting a large ripe red berry and rubbing it against her cheeks.

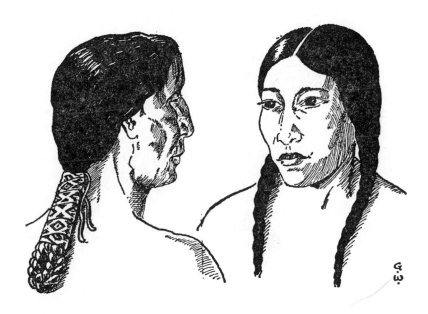

Although the Iroquois spent many hours out-doors, life within the longhouse, which centered around the warmth and companionship of the family quarters and the fire, was always important to them.

4

The Seminole Chikee

THE Seminole Indians of Florida have not existed
as long as other Indian groups. Originally they
were part of the great Creek Confederacy, along
with several other southeastern woodland Indian
tribes. When the Europeans arrived, they wanted
slaves to work on the plantations. Negro slaves
were costly, so they captured many Indians,
especially in Georgia and Alabama. The Indians
did not take kindly to slavery, and they began to

migrate to Florida, which at that time belonged to Spain. Members of such tribes as the Creek, Yuchi, and Hitchiti from Alabama and Georgia, together with Negro and Indian slaves, eventually became the Seminole, a name that did not appear until around 1775. In the language of the Creek, the word is said to mean *runaway* or *separatist*. However, the Seminole themselves claim that it should be pronounced "Se-mi-no'lee," which means *wild*.

After settling in Florida, the Seminole built substantial dwellings similar to those of their white neighbors. They obtained horses and cows and raised crops. Then, in 1818, the white Americans came into Florida, and soon they wanted the Indians' lands. Time after time the army burned their homes. Finally war broke out in 1835 and lasted until 1842, when most of the Seminole were moved to reservations in Oklahoma.

However, one small group of around 300 people refused to go. They fled instead into the Big Cypress Swamp in the Everglades. For a time the American government tried to flush them out, but as the cost of this attempt mounted higher and higher, it at last permitted the Seminole to remain.

The land into which the Indians had fled consisted of sun-hardened pine flats, swamps and marshes, and palmetto barrens, which the white men did not want for themselves. Though the Seminole were completely isolated here, they could support themselves by hunting and fishing and by raising small gardens on the marsh islands. Gradually they developed a whole new culture. Because of the warm climate, they now built their homes without walls, and placed them on stilts, for protection against dampness and against alligators and snakes. Under the floors, or platforms, their pet dogs, pigs, and other domesticated animals found shade during the day and shelter during rain.

These homes were called chikees (chee-kees'). When a chikee rotted and fell apart, it was not difficult to erect a new one, because it was constructed with a minimum of materials. A chikee was rectangular in shape. After roughly marking off a site, the Seminole placed a tall forked post in the ground at each corner. Midway between the corner posts on the longer sides of the rectangle, the builders placed two more poles, opposite each other. They put two taller posts, also forked at the top, midway between the corners on the shorter, or end, sides. In the crotches of these taller posts they rested the ridgepole.

To make the floor, the Indians lashed two long straight poles, two feet off the ground, horizontally along the side poles of the longer walls. On the same level they fastened a third pole, parallel with the ridgepole, between the two taller uprights. Then they made the flooring by lashing split palmetto poles tightly across these crossbeams.

When the floor was finished, the people constructed the roof by laying a pole along the length of the house in the crotches of the three uprights on each side and lashing it into place. At each end of the house they also lashed a pole on the same level to the corner posts and the taller upright. They then fastened thinner poles, which slanted between the lower edge of the roof and

the ridgepole, into place. Next they interwove long, slender saplings lengthwise over and under these rafters until the roof looked much like a large, but loosely woven basket. To these saplings the Indians tied in firmly a thatching of palmetto leaves in an overlapping, rain-shedding pattern. So the roof would stay in place on windy days, they joined logs together in pairs and placed them astraddle over the ridgepole like inverted V's.

Without walls a home was open to sand flies, mosquitoes, and heavy dew. The Seminole solved this problem by using a bed canopy, which was made from a large piece of unbleached muslin and hung from the rafters. Each member of a family had one. In the morning he rolled it up tightly and stored it away under the rafters until he needed it again.

The Indians grouped their chikees around an outdoor living area with a cookhouse in the middle. Built without the usual raised floor, the cookhouse had shelves under the rafters to hold food and extra cooking utensils. Here the women prepared a large pot of meat stew from which all could help themselves at any time. The Seminole observed no regular meals, but simply ate when hungry. Their food included fish, tortoise, wild turkey, and deer, and they also raised pigs and chickens. In the gardens they grew corn, sweet potatoes, pumpkins, and sugarcane. The Seminole harvested wild plums, guavas, and the buds of the cabbage palmetto. In place of drinking water a thin gruel of corn grits, called *sofkee*, always stood

ready in the cookhouse. They pulverized corn in a section of a hollow log with a long, double-ended pestle.

Seminole women prepared food on a large table that was constructed like the chikee floors by lashing split palmetto logs to a frame. Under the sheltering roof of the cookhouse was a long-lasting star fire, like that used in the Ojibwa wigwam. The Seminole used longer, thicker logs than the Ojibwa, but they pointed the butt ends toward a small center blaze, which started them burning, in the same way. As the logs burned away, a woman simply pushed them farther into the center from time to time. The cook placed a pot on the burning ends, and took her ease by sitting on the other end of a log a little back from the flames.

The chikees were used mainly for sleeping and working and for storing personal belongings, but the cookhouse was the center for all the life and activity in a Seminole camp.

5

The Mandan Earth Lodge

THE earth lodge of the Mandan Indians, who are of Siouan linguistic stock, was one of the earliest Indian homes. The Mandans built villages of them, enclosed with strong palisades, along the Missouri River. Up until the eighteenth century, the Cheyenne Indians also occupied such villages. Then they adopted the skin-covered tepee and a roving life.

Constructing an earth lodge was a large undertaking, and all the people who were to occupy it took an active part. If it was well cared for, the lodge would last for a generation of inhabitants. After the Indians had selected a suitable site for the building, one of the men drove a stout peg into the soil. This spot would be the center of the new lodge. The man then tied one end of a long buffalo-hide rope to the peg and fastened another peg to the rope's free end. Pulling the rope tight, he walked a full circle and dug a deep groove into the soil with the end of the peg. The circle he made marked the circumference of the lodge floor. Its diameter was usually twenty to sixty feet, although some lodges measured as much as one hundred feet across.

Within this circle, the Indians dug the earth away, often to a depth of four feet. To the east, where the entrance would be, they scraped out an inward-sloping ramp, six feet wide. Piling all the loosened earth on top of an old buffalo robe, they dragged it outside the circle, so they could use it later.

When the floor space had been excavated, the

Indians scraped it until it was level. After that they poured water over the surface. Once the earth was well saturated, they spread dry grass over it and set it on fire. When the grass had turned to ashes, they repeated the process. Two or three soakings and burnings produced a level floor, baked as hard as clay.

In the center of the floor the Mandans dug a shallow fire pit and lined it with flat stones. This fireplace would be the center for all their indoor social activities, ritual instruction, and work during the winter.

Now the Indians placed peeled poles, with forked branches at the top, around the circle, about eight to ten feet apart. They were the frame for the wall structure. Next they cut the four center posts. Although the lodges were erected with little ceremony, the Mandans did have a ceremony for this part of the construction. They called in an old woman to sing a song over the posts and to pray for the good fortune of the people who would occupy the house. For this service they gave her a good buffalo robe.

The Indians now set up the four poles, which stood fifteen feet high, in a square around the fireplace. Then they laid other poles on top of them from corner to corner in the outline of a square. Next they made long roof poles. The Mandans placed the butt ends of these poles in the forks of the wall uprights and rested the top ends on the horizontal center poles around the fire pit. They then covered the entire structure of the house with several layers of willow rods and a layer of overlapping grass bundles. This was followed by a layer of the excavated earth, which became the outer wall. The people shingled this wall with large strips of sod, stamping them down until they became a solid mass. The grass and seeds in this turf continued to grow, forming a tight waterproof cover over the lodge.

A visitor might easily mistake these grass-covered lodges for large rounded hills from a distance unless he happened to see smoke coming through the smoke hole in the center of the roof.

To help keep out drafts in winter, the Mandans added a long hall, leading into the entrance ramp, to the lodge. It had slender, upright side walls and a flat roof, also covered with earth. They made a door from a stiff buffalo hide, lashed to a sapling frame, to cover the entrance, and hung a curtain of soft tanned skins over the inner entrance.

Several families, all belonging to the same clan, shared one lodge. Each household had its own section, which was walled off by a partition. The partitions were made with poles, skins, and rush mats. Each room had a low platform inside for sleeping. The Mandans covered the platforms with buffalo robes, tanned with the hair left on for added warmth. On very cold nights the people hung skin curtains around the outside of their sleeping quarters for insulation.

All the women sharing a single lodge owned it jointly. To them also belonged the household items such as bedding, clay pots, baskets, and garden tools. Even the travois dogs, the gardens, and the mares and colts from the horse herds were theirs. The men owned their own weapons, as well as the stallions and geldings. During the cold months the men brought their best war and buffalo horses into the lodge and stabled them to the left of the entrance.

The daily life of these women was easier than that of the woman who lived in a one-family lodge. The young girls learned how to cure meat, to till the gardens, and to observe all the proper tribal rituals by doing these things with the older women.

In late spring, summer, and early fall, the

people conducted most of their activities outdoors, usually on top of their grass-covered earth homes. This roof was an ideal place for the smaller children to play, for here they were out of the way of men riding through the village. Lookouts, stationed on these high mounds, also had a fine view of the surrounding landscape.

In the center of each earth-lodge village was a large open space that the people used as an arena for ceremonies, dances, and powwows. When the head man of a lodge was elected as a chief or a ceremonial leader, his neighbors expected him to give a feast. Therefore, as soon as the village crier, or herald, made the news public, the elected man went hunting with the other men of his lodge. When they returned with game, the women went to work, roasting the meat and gathering bulbs and roots, and made the feast ready.

The Mandan Indians observed many such ceremonies throughout the year. They lived a communal life in and around the earth lodges for two or more centuries until at last, around 1880, they stopped using them.

6

The Pueblo Adobe

SCIENTISTS believe that the cliff dwellers of the arid Southwest were the ancestors of the present-day Pueblo Indians. The first homes of the cliff dwellers were deep caves, often protected by an overhanging ledge, high in the sides of the sandstone cliffs. Woven cloth, storage pits, kivas, and the remains of their living quarters still exist. Below the cliff houses they cultivated fields, where they raised corn, squash, beans, and cotton. Sometimes the fields were at a river's edge. If not, the cliff dwellers irrigated them.

Trails led from the fields to the edge of the cliff. From there the people climbed up by means of ladders and toe holds. The ladders were notched logs, set up wherever the cliffsides were particularly steep. Where the cliffsides sloped more gently, the cliff dwellers cut toe and finger notches into the sandstone. When a person needed to transport something up or down, he carried it in a burden basket on his back or balanced it on his head, for he had to have both hands free for climbing. In case of a raid, the cliff dwellers retreated to their stronghold, pulling up the ladders after them.

Whenever enough rain fell, the Indians raised a surplus crop and stored it away for leaner times. They made storage rooms by digging round or square bins deep in the cave floor and lining them with flat rocks. When the bins were full of food, they covered them with large lids, made from woven branches and clay. The lids protected the food and prevented accidents.

As time passed, the cave population grew. The people needed more living space, so they began to build homes. From measurements of tree rings found in their building timbers, we know these homes were built as early as 1103 A.D. The cliff dwellers made rooms as they had made storage bins, but built them above the cave floor. These rooms were rectangular in shape and constructed of wood, stones, and clay. Logs spanned the walls, making a flat roof. Across the logs the Indians placed saplings and brush and then covered the roof with a thick layer of clay, as they had made the storage covers. When the need arose, they built smaller rooms on top of the first, the roof of the room below providing a floor for the upper room.

These early homes had no doors, but were entered through a roof hatch. To gain entrance, an Indian had to climb a notched-log ladder to the roof, and then climb down another ladder from the hatch to the interior. A small opening under the rafters provided light and air. For the most part, however, these rooms were only used as sleeping quarters and as a place to keep a few personal belongings. The people did their work and cooking outdoors.

In time the growing community became an organized society. To keep order, the cliff dwellers chose elders and priests, and they became prominent and respected leaders. The people dug ceremonial chambers, called kivas, below the cave floors. The kivas were large circular rooms, entered from above, and they served also as the men's clubrooms and sleeping quarters. In the early days, even the married men slept in them. We know that the religious life of these Indians was very important because of the number of kivas that have been found in the ruins of these villages.

Then this ancient tribe suddenly vanished. We do not know yet just what took place. There was one period, however, when the Southwest was caught in the grip of a continuous drought for twenty-three years. Perhaps this calamity made the cliff dwellers move away, but we still do not know where they went. We feel certain that at least some of these people returned, because the culture of the twentieth-century Pueblo Indians can be traced back to that of the early cliff dwellers.

The villages of the Pueblo Indians, whether on mesa tops or in flat country, were here long before the Spaniards came. Although we speak of these villagers as the Pueblo Indians, they are not one tribe. They all lived in pueblos, which is the Spanish word for towns, but each group had its own individual language, its own crafts, and its own ceremonies and dances. Some of the well-known Pueblo people are the Hopi, the Zuñi, and the Acoma. The oldest pueblo is the Hopi village of Oraibi, which was built in 1150 A.D. and has been continually inhabited since then.

Although the Pueblo houses were alike in general, there were differences in detail from village to village. This was also true of the village kivas. Today the Hopi kiva is a rectangular, four-cornered room. In the village of the Acoma it is circular. The kiva in Taos is completely underground, and in San Ildefonso and Santo Domingo the kivas are built partly above and partly below the ground.

The homes of the Pueblo were much like those of the cliff dwellers, except that they were in open country. In some villages they were only one or two stories high; in others they were five stories high. The houses were divided into rooms much as ours are today, but since the entrance was on the rooftop, the general rooms were above and the sleeping rooms below.

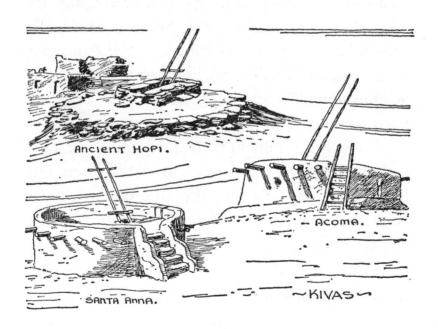

The men and women worked together building a home. The men brought, often from a great distance, the logs and poles used for wall supports and for rafters. After the framework had been erected, the women built up the stone walls and covered them with wet adobe. When the home was finished, it became the property of the women.

The women also planned the room interior. Originally they built their fire in an open pit in the center of the family room. In those days the smoke escaped through the entrance of the house, which was on the roof. Gradually the women began to build the fireplace in the corner of the room instead. Over it they placed a long flue that reached up through the rafters. After the fireplace had been completed, a woman added a clay chimney pot on the roof. Now, when a fire was going indoors, the smoke went up and out the chimney pot, leaving the entrance to the room free and clear of smoke.

Wood for the fires rarely grew nearby. It was, therefore, a custom that anyone coming back to the village brought wood with him, especially if he had no other burden to carry. The Pueblo also used dried corncobs as a fuel.

The homelife of these Indians was, and is, one of great closeness. During the summer months the family arose early. At the first sign of day the grandfather went up to greet the dawn. Near the edge of the roof he stood and sang to the sunrise, sprinkling pollen or cornmeal as a prayer to the Dawn People.

Down below in the sleeping rooms the rest of the family stirred. High up, suspended from the rafters, was a long pole—the "pole of soft goods." Over it the people draped the blankets and robes on which they had been sleeping. Then one of the women made the room ready for the day by sweeping it with a broom made from yucca fibers.

The older boys took off for the river to bathe. Little children and adults washed at home in water brought from the river or from a nearby spring. Afterward the men started for the fields, carrying with them some food left over from the day before, for they did not eat breakfast.

When the women started the fire, they were ready to begin the daily chores. First there was corn to grind and then food to prepare for the big evening meal. Along one of the inner walls of the family room were three corn-grinding bins, built so that there was just enough space between them and the wall for a person to kneel while working. Each of the three bins had a grinding slab. The roughest was a coarse slab of lava. The second was made of sandstone, ground down to a medium coarseness. The third was also of sandstone, but had a finer surface.

Three women ground the corn with rounded stones that looked like stone rolling pins without handles. Each stone was as long as the bin was wide. The first woman broke up the shelled corn on the rough lava slab. After grinding it with the stone, she pushed it into a waiting tray or basket and passed it on to the woman working at the medium slab, who ground it again until it was a fine meal. The second woman passed the meal on to the third, who ground the corn down in her bin

until she had a very fine, fluffy corn flour. To grind a supply of this fine flour for several days took the whole morning. While working, the women often sang the ancient corn-grinding songs, which made light of the work and also helped to pass the time. Sometimes one of the old men joined them and accompanied their songs with his reed flute.

The men had to work hard to grow enough food and the women had to work hard to prepare it, so the Pueblo were careful never to waste any. They were grateful for their meals and blessed them by taking a small portion of food and dropping it into

the fire. In this way, they invited their protecting gods to come and eat with them.

There were other interesting Indian homes in the Southwest too. The sheep-herding Navaho lived in hogans, which were very much like small Mandan earth lodges. These single-family dwellings were built with logs, poles, branches, and brush, and were also covered with earth.

The western Apache lived in small bands, their homes well hidden within easily defended rocky fortresses, for the Apache were fighting men. Their homes, called wickiups, were circular in shape, with domed roofs. They were from five to seven feet high and from six to ten feet in diameter. The Apache constructed their wickiups from poles and brush.

All of these homes were well suited to the life and climate of the Southwest.

7
The Plank House

PRIDE in manhood, in war and hunting exploits, and in a good name was common among Indian tribes. Most were modest about their great deeds, and let others tell about them, but the Northwest Coast Indians were an exception. These people lived under a rigid caste system, made up of aristocrats, a middle class, and slaves. If a youngster belonged to a high-standing family in the village, he was not brought up to be modest. Instead he was taught to be arrogant.

People who were related by birth or marriage lived together in large plank houses. The house posts and door poles were carved and painted with the crests of the high-ranking members of the families who lived in them. In the villages of the Nootka, the plank houses stood in long rows on high ground, all facing the calm waters of an inlet. The sound of the ocean was always in their ears. On some days they might hear a soft lapping of the waters flowing over the beach. On other days they heard the high roar of great whitecaps hurling themselves against the rocks and breaking. From the time a child was able to walk, he was near, in, or on these waters.

The coastal climate was usually mild, and the region abounded in cedar and spruce, from which came the material the Nootka used to build their homes. The cedars grew very straight, and an Indian could split the wood from them easily and evenly with his stone and antler-bone tools. First he had to cut the tree down, unless it had blown over in a storm, as sometimes happened. He notched the tree with his stone ax on the side facing the direction in which he wanted it to fall. Then he drove hardwood or antler wedges into the tree from the opposite side until it toppled.

To produce planks for his house, the Indian hammered wedges into the felled tree in a straight line from end to end, following the grain of the wood, and thus split it. He needed many planks, for the average house was seventy-five feet long and twenty-five feet wide. The homes were rectangular, and were constructed with a strong frame of cedar posts. Crossbeams, also of cedar, rested on top of the posts. The Nootka made the roof and the walls from the long cedar planks. In some of the houses the planks were placed vertically. In others they ran horizontally.

Lower-ranking families entered their homes through an opening between the planks. Over it they hung a reed mat. There was also an additional opening at the far end, which saved time when someone wanted to enter from that direction. This opening also served as an escape route to the forest, in case of raids.

High-ranking families entered their homes

through more elaborate doorways. In front of each of their houses was an enormous totem pole. It was erected flush against the front wall and stood higher than the ridgepole. A family set up a totem pole, with its many carved figures of birds and animals, in memory of an ancestor. A figure at the bottom might represent a large beaver, carved in an upright sitting position, its flat tail held tightly against its body. Within the outline of this tail, the Indians would cut a hole through the totem pole and through the plank wall. Through this unusual doorway the people entered and left the house.

As soon as a visitor entered the house, he had a full view of its roomy interior. The back wall was decorated with two large thunderbirds, painted in bright colors. At this end were the living quarters of the clan chief and his family. From floor to ridgepole stood another totem pole, flanked by two big, deeply carved storage boxes. Built against the side walls, to the left and right of these boxes, were the sleeping quarters, enclosed with cattail mats to give them privacy. The

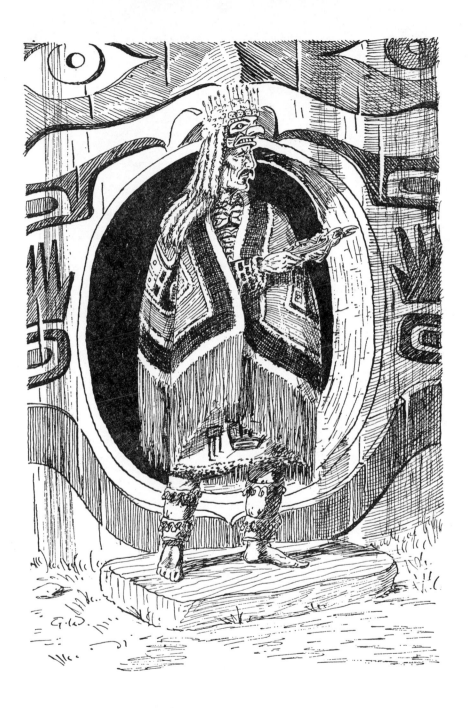

sleeping quarters were built-up platforms, with large storage shelves above them.

Close relatives, though some were of lesser rank, all occupied this one building. Each family unit had a section of its own. They divided the sections from one another with plank walls, adorned with totemic figures of birds, animals, whales, and fishes. All the families had slaves, men and women captured during raids on other villages, and they placed their slaves' sleeping platforms in front of and below their own. During the day they used these low platforms as benches.

In the middle of the room was a rectangular pit about five feet deep. In it the Nootka arranged several fires for heat, light, and cooking. Usually from two to five family units shared one fire. Suspended from the rafters over the fires were racks upon which the people dried and smoked fish. They made a smoke hole above the racks by simply pushing aside a loose roof board. Fish was their chief food, and they ate it boiled, steamed, roasted, or smoked.

The Nootka were fine craftsmen. They worked

on many of their crafts indoors by the fire, either in bad weather or during the evenings. They painted designs on house boards and on paddle blades, and carved fine wooden masks, rattles, fish clubs, or house posts.

Social rank determined the seating of family members at a ceremony or at a potlatch. When a potlatch was given for a chief from another village, his family, and his tribesmen, proper seating and respect for rank were of the utmost importance, because a breach of etiquette could cause a war.

The word *potlatch* comes from the Chinook word *patshatl,* which means *giving.* Any occasion for celebration could turn into a potlatch. A chief might want to celebrate the birth of a son, a high-ranking family might give a coming-out party for a daughter, or a village might want to honor a dead chief. Perhaps the occasion for the greatest potlatch came when two villages merged, as often happened. The host gave away beautiful blankets, carved cedar chests, and valuable furs, to gain prestige for himself and to belittle his visitors. As the chiefs kept slaves, it was not uncommon for the potlatch giver to kill one or two of them, to show his rival that he had so many slaves he would not miss them. During these rituals, which were carried out with great dignity, he and his guests sang songs of insult to each other.

Hundreds of guests were invited to a big potlatch, and there was not enough room to house them in the plank homes of the village. Instead the Nootka built special potlatch houses. The potlatch houses were much like the family dwellings,

CARVED BOX, FUR, AND A "SLAVE KILLER"

but they did not have divided sleeping quarters. Carved interior house posts held up the rafters, and the inside walls were decorated with painted family crests of ravens, whales, beavers, and other figures. Around the upper walls the villagers hung several "coppers," which were large copper plates, hammered out and painted with the crests of the owners. They were of great value—one might be worth several hundred blankets. Seats for the high-ranking guests were carved and painted, as were the big storage boxes that were given to

"COPPERS"

the visitors to hold their blankets, furs, and other valuables.

An outstanding feature of the potlatch house was the great serving bowl, which was carved from a single cedar log. It measured up to eight feet in length and was hollowed out in the center. A craftsman might carve it to represent a reclining human figure or perhaps a whale. The server scooped food from this large bowl into smaller, but equally well-carved bowls for the slaves to carry to the diners. The serving spoons, either of

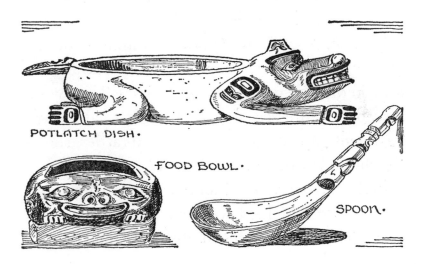

POTLATCH DISH.

FOOD BOWL.

SPOON.

wood or of bone, had carved handles, and each well-to-do family reserved a set of them especially for guests.

The finest clothes were worn at a potlatch. In their daily village life, the men dressed in little more than breechclouts. At a potlatch, however, they wore large, heavy hats, carved from cedar and inlaid with a shell design representing the clan totem of the wearer. The nobles also wore highly decorated, loose-hanging shirts and skin or cloth leggings that reached from below the knees to the ankles. Each clan leader carried in his hand a carved staff, not unlike a tall, slender totem pole. At ceremonials he was never seen without it. A knife in his belt and a club, known as the "slave killer," completed his outfit. The women dressed in wrap-around skirts. They wore carved headdresses, copper bracelets, and shell ornaments, and often carried carved rattles, showing their clan totem.

Potlatches were costly affairs, and a really grand one could not be held with one man's belongings alone. Therefore, a chief borrowed from the vil-

lagers everything of value they had to offer. He then had to repay all the borrowed goods within a year, usually with interest. In this way, a potlatch actually became a village affair, and all the villagers won or lost face, depending on the outcome.

After giving a potlatch, a man hoped that his rival could not possibly outdo him. If the return potlatch was more lavish, however, the loser could no longer face the people of his village. Then he went off to war and deliberately fought in a position where he was sure to be slain.

8
The Indian Home Today

THE homelife of many Indians today is much the same as it was years ago. For others it has changed drastically.

The Algonquian wigwam still exists in some parts of the northern forests, but many Ojibwa families now live in frame houses on reservations. These houses are small and usually no warmer than the old-time wigwam. Some Ojibwa work as guides for sportsmen, hunting and trapping, and live much as their grandfathers once did. The guide's home is often a well-built log cabin, situated by a lake or a stream. He may also have an extra shed for wood, tools, and canoes.

The Iroquois of today live on reservations throughout upper New York and Canada. Most of them have single-family frame houses or log cabins, some of which are two stories high. Modern longhouses are used only for ceremonies and are made of logs instead of a bark-covered frame.

The Florida Seminole still occupy the chikee. They are self-reliant, and cling in many respects to their old ways. Their children attend government schools on the reservation. The men hunt, fish, and care for their own small gardens. Some guide hunting parties, while others catch frogs in great numbers, so they can sell the legs to the Miami restaurants.

The women use hand-operated sewing machines to make colorful sport shirts for men and skirts for women. Today the Seminole find a growing market for them among the tourists. Visitors are welcome in the Seminole villages, except during the times when the Indians hold their special tribal ceremonies.

The people of the earth lodge are no more. Their culture changed, and they became nomadic buffalo hunters. Today these Indians live on reservations in frame houses, in tar-paper shacks, or in small cabins, built from old railroad ties.

The Pueblo Indians live much as they always have. The adobe houses now have windows and ordinary doors, like other houses, but the Indians usually paint the doors and window frames a bright turquoise blue. Inside they now have real beds with springs and mattresses, and often there is a gaily patterned linoleum on the floor. However, at mealtime the family will sit down on the clean floor, in a ring around the common food bowl, and eat the same way they have for centuries.

Most of the old totem poles of the Northwest Indians have fallen down, and can be seen today only in museums. The large plank houses and the potlatch houses have also gone. The families now

NORTHWEST COAST.

OKLAHOMA

DAKOTA

NEW YORK STATE

G.W

live in small frame homes, each containing a single family unit.

By the late 1890's the Indian population on the reservations numbered about 300,000. Today this number has reached nearly 450,000. Most of the Indians who wish to cling to the traditional ways of the past have gone to the Sandhills, the Happy Hunting Grounds, and with them has disappeared much of the old culture. The modern Indian is changing with the times and lives more and more as other Americans do.

Appendix

BELOW is a list of the better-known tribes belonging to the linguistic groups shown on the map on page 8. The tribes discussed in the foregoing chapters are listed in italic type.

ALGONQUIAN

Ojibwa, Cree, Micmac, Delaware, Shawnee, Menomini, Blackfeet, Cheyenne, Arapaho.

IROQUOIAN

Iroquois, Cherokee.

SOUTHEAST

The Creek and their confederacy to which the *Seminole* originally belonged spoke the Muskogean language. After the Seminole settled in Florida, their languages, of which there are two, were the Timucuan and Calusa. They are isolated languages, and the Seminole group that speaks one cannot understand the other.

SIOUAN

Mandan, Sioux, Osage, Crow, Catawba, Winnebago.

ATHABASKAN

Pueblo, Navaho, Apache, Kiowa Apache, and several tribes in northern Canada, including the Chipewyan.

NORTHWEST COAST

Many languages were spoken here, and so a common "trade" language, known as Chinook, came into use. Some of the tribes in this group were: *Nootka,* Haida, Tlingit, Kwakiutl.

95

INDEX

* Indicates illustrations